DETROIT
TIGERS
STARS, STATS, HISTORY, AND MORE!
BY K. C. KELLEY

The Child's World®
childsworld.com

Published by The Child's World®
1980 Lookout Drive • Mankato, MN 56003-1705
800-599-READ • www.childsworld.com

ISBN 9781503828230
LCCN 2018944836

Printed in the United States of America
PA02392

Photo Credits:
Cover: Joe Robbins (2)
Interior: AP Images: 17, Jim Mone 19; Library of
Congress: 9; Newscom: Richard Tsong-Taatarli/TNS 10,
Adam Jacobs/Icon SMI BAN 20; Nick Wosicka/Icon SW
27; Joe Robbins 5, 6, 13, 14, 23, 24, 29.

About the Author

K.C. Kelley is a huge sports
fan who has written more
than 100 books for kids. His
favorite sport is baseball.
He has also written about
football, basketball, soccer,
and even auto racing! He lives
in Santa Barbara, California.

On the Cover

Main photo: Miguel Cabrera;
Inset: Al Kaline, "Mr. Tiger"

CONTENTS

GO, TIGERS!

T he Detroit Tigers are one of baseball's oldest teams. They have been making their fans happy for almost 120 years! Tigers fans have seen **World Series** champions and **Hall of Fame** superstars. They have stayed with their team through tough times, too. Today's Tigers hope to add to their great history. Let's meet the Tigers!

Detroit fans have loved watching Miguel Cabrera. ➤
He is one of the top hitters of all time.

WHO ARE THE TIGERS?

Detroit plays in the American League (AL). That group is part of Major League Baseball (MLB). MLB also includes the National League (NL). There are 30 teams in MLB. The winner of the AL plays the winner of the NL in the World Series.

◀ *Pitcher Michael Fulmer is a big part of the Tigers' future.*

WHERE THEY CAME FROM

The Detroit Tigers first played in the Western League from 1894 to 1900. In 1901, that league became the AL. The Tigers were part of the AL from that very first season. They are one of only two AL teams to keep the same home city and team name since the start. Thirteen Hall of Fame players spent most of their careers with Detroit.

Ty Cobb is one of only two MLB players ➤
with more than 4,000 career hits.

COBB DETROIT

9

WHO THEY PLAY

The Tigers play in the AL Central Division. The other teams in the AL Central are the Chicago White Sox, the Cleveland Indians, the Kansas City Royals, and the Minnesota Twins. The Tigers play more games against their division **rivals** than against other teams. In all, the Tigers play 162 games each season. They play 81 games at home and 81 on the road.

◄ *Detroit's Nick Castellanos slides into second against the AL Central's Twins.*

WHERE THEY PLAY

Comerica Park is heaven for Tigers fans. Fans can see statues of their heroes. They can ride on a Ferris wheel. The wheel's cars are shaped like baseballs! Kids can ride a carousel of tigers. Inside, fans get a great view of the field and the Detroit **skyline**.

A huge stone tiger inspires fans as they enter Comerica Park. ➤

THE BASEBALL FIELD

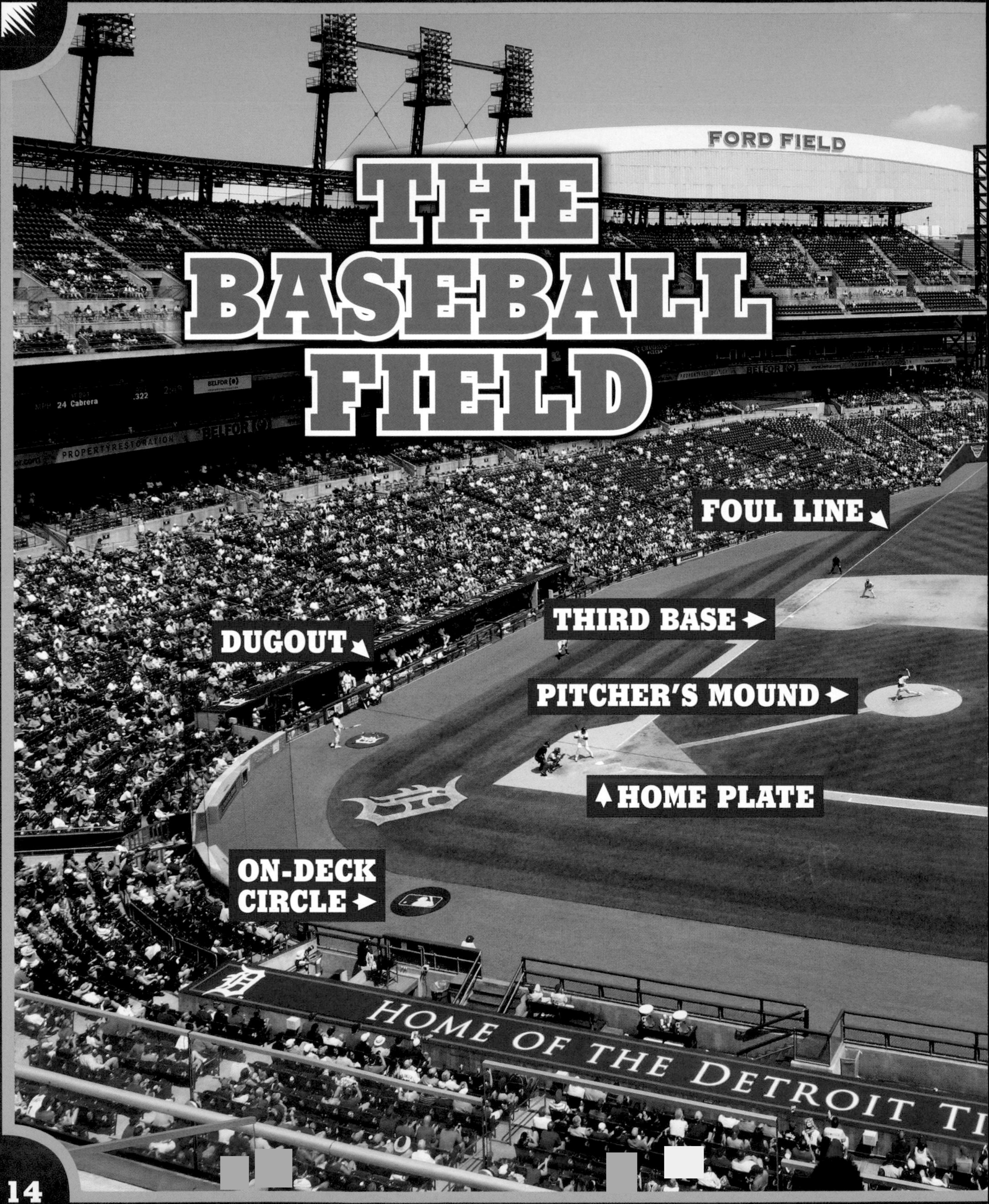

FORD FIELD

FOUL LINE ➤

THIRD BASE ➤

DUGOUT ➤

PITCHER'S MOUND ➤

▲ HOME PLATE

ON-DECK CIRCLE ➤

HOME OF THE DETROIT TI

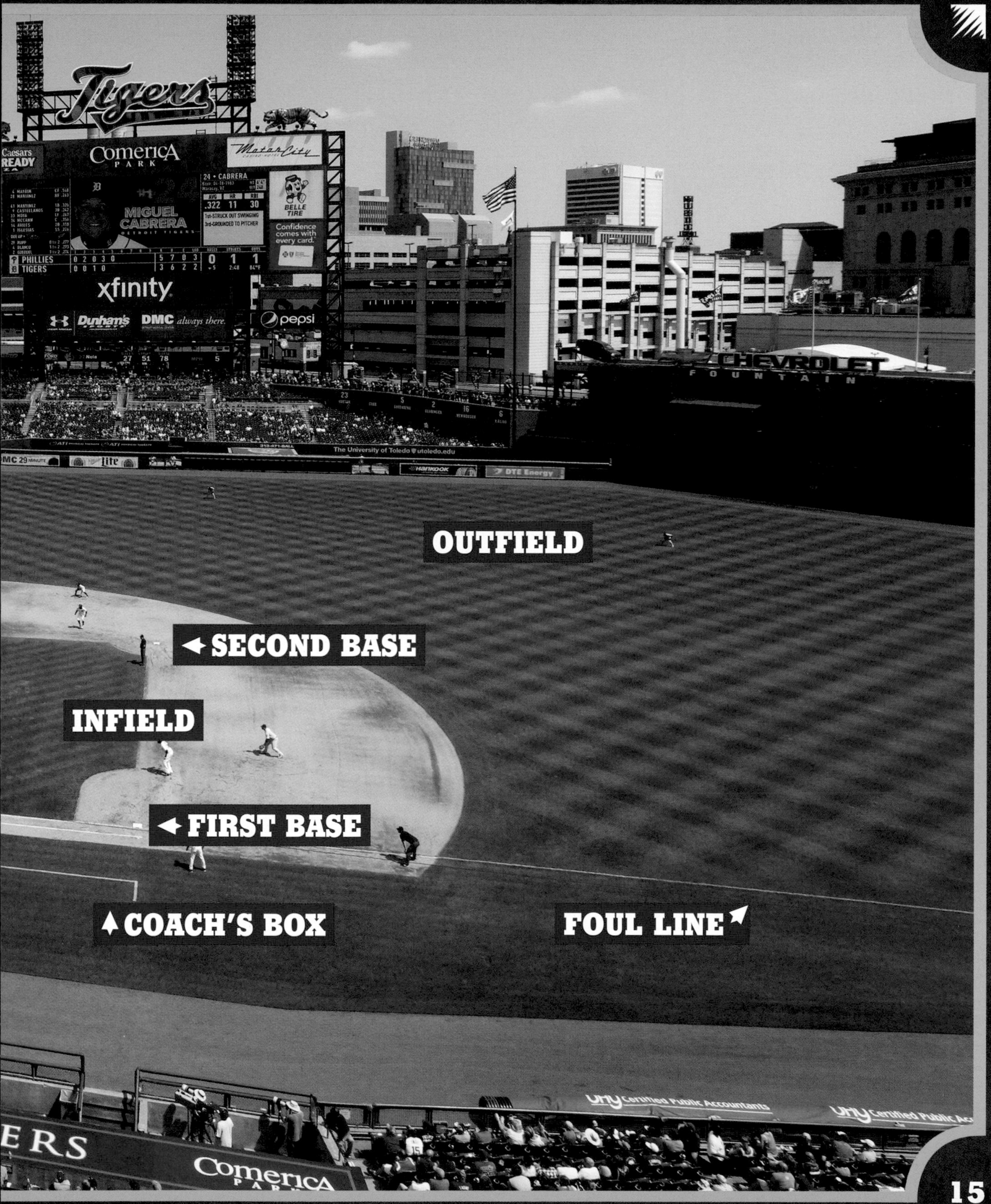

OUTFIELD

SECOND BASE

INFIELD

FIRST BASE

COACH'S BOX

FOUL LINE

BIG DAYS

The Tigers have had a lot of great days in their long history. Here are a few of them.

1935—Hank Greenberg led the AL with 36 homers and 168 **runs batted in**. He led Detroit to its first World Series title.

1984—What a start! The Tigers set an MLB record by opening the season with 35 wins in their first 40 games. Detroit also won the World Series.

2012—The Tigers won another AL **pennant**. They beat the New York Yankees in the playoffs. Detroit lost the World Series, but it was a great season!

The Tigers danced for joy after they won the 1984 World Series. ➤

TOUGH DAYS

Like every team, the Tigers have had some not-so-great days, too.

1909—Detroit made its third straight World Series. And it lost its third straight World Series!

2003—What happened to the Tigers? The team hit bottom this season. It lost a club-record 119 games!

2009— The Tigers and Twins finished with the same record. The two teams had to play a one-game playoff. Minnesota won in the twelfth inning, making Tigers fans sad.

Brandon Inge didn't win this argument with the umpire. ➤
Detroit didn't win the 2009 playoff game, either!

MEET THE FANS!

A few seasons ago, Tigers fans saw their team in the playoffs four years in a row! The last couple of seasons have not been as good. The fans stay loyal, though. **Attendance** has been more than 2.3 million every year since 2006! At the ballpark, a giant tiger **mascot** named Paws helps fans cheer.

◄ *Paws shows off his dance moves on top of the Tigers dugout.*

HEROES THEN

The Tigers' long history has included many Hall of Fame stars. Ty Cobb had 4,189 hits. That's the second-most of all time. His .366 batting average is No. 1 overall. In the 1930s, Hank Greenberg was one of baseball's best home run hitters. In the 1960s, Al Kaline combined great hitting with top outfield defense. In the 1980s, Kirk Gibson, Alan Trammell, and Lou Whitaker helped the Tigers win two division titles. Now with Houston, Justin Verlander won the MVP and the **Cy Young Award** with Detroit.

Al Kaline played his whole 22-year career with Detroit. ➤

HEROES NOW

The Tigers have a mix of young and veteran stars. Third baseman Nick Castellanos is a solid hitter. He should be a star for many years. Shortstop Jose Iglesias plays great defense and can steal bases. When he is healthy, Miguel Cabrera is one of the top hitters of all time. Young Michael Fulmer is the key to the Tigers pitching staff.

◄ *Nick Castellanos shows off his skill on the basepaths.*

GEARING UP

Baseball players wear team uniforms. On defense, they wear leather gloves to catch the ball. As batters, they wear hard helmets. This protects them from pitches. Batters hit the ball with long wood bats. Each player chooses his own size of bat. Catchers have the toughest job. They wear a lot of protection.

THE BASEBALL

The outside of the Major League baseball is made from cow leather. Two leather pieces shaped like 8s are stitched together. There are 108 stitches of red thread. These stitches help players grip the ball. Inside, the ball has a small center of cork and rubber. Hundreds of feet of yarn are tightly wound around this center.

CATCHER'S MASK
AND HELMET

CHEST
PROTECTOR ►

CATCHER'S
MITT

◄ WRIST
BANDS

◄ SHIN GUARDS

CATCHER'S GEAR

TEAM STATS

Here are some of the all-time career records for the Detroit Tigers. All these stats are through the 2018 regular season.

HOME RUNS

Al Kaline	399
Norm Cash	373

RBI

Ty Cobb	1,811
Al Kaline	1,582

BATTING AVERAGE

Ty Cobb	.368
Harry Heilmann	.342

STOLEN BASES

Ty Cobb	869
Donie Bush	402

WINS

Hooks Dauss	223
George Mullin	209

SAVES

Todd Jones	235
Mike Henneman	154

He's with Houston in 2019, but Justin Verlander ➤
had many great years in Detroit.

STRIKEOUTS	
Mickey Lolich	2,679
Justin Verlander	2,373

GLOSSARY

attendance (uh-TEN-dence) a measure of how many people go to a sports event

Cy Young Award (SY YUNG uh-WARD) an honor given to the top pitcher in each league

Hall of Fame (HALL UV FAYM) a building in Cooperstown, New York, that honors baseball greats

mascot (MASS-kot) a costumed character that entertains fans

pennant (PEN-nunt) a triangle-shaped cloth given to a team for winning a league championship

rivals (RYE-vuhlz) two people or groups competing for the same thing

runs batted in (RBI) (RUNZ BAT-ted IN) a stat that counts each time a batter causes a player (including himself) to score

skyline (SKY-lyn) the shape of a city's tall buildings as seen from a distance

World Series (WURLD SEE-reez) the annual championship of Major League Baseball

FIND OUT MORE

IN THE LIBRARY

Aretha, David. *12 Reasons to Love the Detroit Tigers*. Mankato, MN: 12-Story Library, 2016.

Connery-Boyd, Peg. *Detroit Tigers: Big Book of Activities*. Chicago, IL: Sourcebooks/Jabberwocky, 2016.

Rhodes, Sam. *Detroit Tigers (Inside MLB)*. Calgary, AB: Weigl, 2018.

ON THE WEB

Visit our website for links about the Detroit Tigers:
childsworld.com/links

Note to Parents, Teachers, and Librarians: We routinely verify our web links to make sure they are safe and active sites. So encourage your readers to check them out!

INDEX